THIS PUPPY BOOK BELONGS TO:
_____

_____

I am -------------- Years Old

Welcome

to the "Little Hands Coloring Series" for toddlers!

If you like this puppy dog coloring book,
please take a minute or so and
leave a review on Amazon.
We will bark with delight!

tiny.cc/puppyrev

It really makes a difference!

Thank you,
Julie

Bonus Pages

More toddler fun,
FREE DOWNLOAD!
tiny.cc/puppybonus

YOU DRAW

YOU DRAW

YOU DRAW

YOU DRAW

YOU DRAW

YOU DRAW

YOU DRAW

YOU DRAW

YOU DRAW

YOU DRAW

YOU DRAW

YOU DRAW

YOU DRAW

YOU DRAW

YOU DRAW

YOU DRAW

YOU DRAW

YOU DRAW

YOU DRAW

YOU DRAW

YOU DRAW

YOU DRAW

YOU DRAW

YOU DRAW

YOU DRAW

YOU DRAW

YOU DRAW

YOU DRAW

YOU DRAW

YOU DRAW

YOU DRAW

YOU DRAW

YOU DRAW

YOU DRAW

YOU DRAW

YOU DRAW

YOU DRAW

YOU DRAW

YOU DRAW

YOU DRAW

YOU DRAW

YOU DRAW

YOU DRAW

YOU DRAW

YOU DRAW

YOU DRAW

YOU DRAW

YOU DRAW

We hope your toddler is having great fun coloring all the Puppies!

Picturing the toddlers happily having fun and building skills with a book we made is a giant part of what makes us smile. Thinking about those big smiles and the refrigerator pictures is a big reward for us. We strive to keep that magic in all the children's books we set about creating here at Dibble Dabble Press.

*Check out the other fun and skill building books in
"The Little Hands Coloring Series" just for Toddlers
and all our Activity and Handwriting Practice Books made special, just for the kids.*

The Little Hands Coloring Series

mybook.to/ToddlerSeries

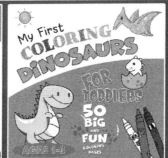

mybook.to/SketchDDP

mybook.to/DDPSketch

* LINKS ARE CASE SENSTIVE

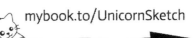

mybook.to/UnicornSketch

mybook.to/UnicornDDP

mybook.to/SketchPad

mybook.to/Big

mybook.to/BooSketch

mybook.to/BooActivity

mybook.to/playandlearn

mybook.to/BooColor

mybook.to/MyDino

mybook.to/Practice

LINKS ARE CASE SENSTIVE

mybook.to/Number

mybook.to/FunGratitude

mybook.to/RainbowSketch

If you liked your book in this
"Little Hands Coloring Series"
please take a minute or so and
leave us a review

tiny.cc/puppyrev

Thank you,
Julie

amazon.com/dibbledabblepress

Julie@dibbledabblepress.com

Made in the USA
Las Vegas, NV
17 December 2024

14549997R00057